AMAZING OLYMPIC RECORDS

BY PAUL HOBLIN

The Child's World

Published by The Child's World®
1980 Lookout Drive • Mankato, MN 56003-1705
800-599-READ • www.childsworld.com

Acknowledgments
The Child's World®: Mary Berendes, Publishing Director
The Design Lab: Design
Amnet: Production
Red Line Editorial: Editorial direction

Design Elements: iStockPhoto

Photographs ©: Michael Probst/AP Images, cover, 11;
Peter Macdiarmid/Getty Images, 5; Julio Cortez/AP
Images, 7; AP Images, 9; Pete Niesen/Shutterstock
Images, 13; Roberto Borea/AP Images, 15; Thomas Kienzle/
AP Images, 17; Kyodo/AP Images, 19; Itsuo Inouye/AP
Images, 21; Kyodo/AP Images, 23; Charles Dharapak/AP
Images, 25; Edgar R. Schoepal/AP Images, 27; Bettmann/
Corbis/AP Images, 29

ISBN 9781614734055
LCCN 2012946500

Printed in the United States of America
Mankato, MN
November, 2012
PA02146

Disclaimer: The information in this book is current
through the 2012 London Olympic Games.

ABOUT THE AUTHOR
**Paul Hoblin has written several
sports books. He has an MFA from
the University of Minnesota. He
plays many different sports.**

TABLE OF
CONTENTS

ONE

A 2,700-YEAR-OLD IDEA

The first Olympics took place in 776 BC in the Greek city Olympia. The games were part of a religious festival that honored Zeus. He was the king of the gods in Greek mythology. Greek cities, called city-states, were often at war with each other. But during the Olympics, all of Greece agreed to a truce. This meant there was no war. People could travel safely to the games.

Many of the events of the ancient Olympics were similar to ones we have today. Athletes ran, wrestled, and threw the **discus** and the **javelin**. Ancient Greeks also had a long jump competition. There were some differences from the modern long jump, though. Back then athletes did not take running starts like they do today. However, they were allowed to use **halteres**. Long jumpers held these weighted objects in their hands. Before they jumped, the athletes swung the halteres behind them. Doing this helped them jump farther.

FOUNDING THE OLYMPIC GAMES

Olympia is located in the western part of the Peloponnese area in Greece. The Peloponnese is named after King Pelops. According to Greek myth, either Pelops or his great-grandson Herakles founded the Olympic Games.

A Greek vase from 540 BC shows an athlete taking part in the long jump in the ancient Olympics.

THE MODERN OLYMPICS

The modern Olympic Games began in 1896 AD. Once again, these games were held in Greece. The games included athletes from many countries around the world. Today, more than 10,000 athletes from 200 or more countries go for the gold in each Olympics. The summer and winter Olympics are now held in different countries, as well.

No athlete has won more gold medals in a single Olympics than Michael Phelps did in 2008. Going into the games that year, Phelps was already considered the best swimmer in the world. At the 2004 summer Olympics, he won six gold medals. But Phelps was not satisfied. Another U.S. swimmer named Mark Spitz had set the all-time record for gold medals in a single Olympics at seven. Spitz set the record back in 1972.

In an incredibly close race, Phelps won his seventh gold medal when he was declared the winner by 4/100ths of a second. His record-breaking eighth gold was not as close. But he had some help from his teammates that time. Phelps swam one leg of a four-man relay. Together the team finished first.

MORE MEDALS FOR PHELPS
Entering the 2012 Olympics in London, Michael Phelps already had more medals than any other man in Olympic history. By the time he left the 2012 games, he had more medals than any other athlete in Olympic history. His 22 medals broke the old record of 18.

SPITZ SETS RECORD
Mark Spitz won every swimming event he entered in the 1972 Olympics. Not only was Spitz a perfect seven for seven, he also set world records in all seven events.

Michael Phelps swims in a race during the 2012 summer Olympics in London on August 4, 2012.

TWO

AMAZING OLYMPIANS

Some records are quickly broken, but there are others that stand the test of time. Perhaps no record is more amazing than the one that long jumper Bob Beamon set in 1968. Beamon jumped so far that he out-jumped the measuring equipment. Olympic officials had to use a regular tape measure to figure out just how far he had jumped. They finally announced his distance: 29.2 feet (8.9 m). Beamon fell to the ground in disbelief. He broke the old record by almost 2 feet (0.6 m).

THE LOCOMOTIVE

Czech athlete Emil Zatopek was one of the greatest runners of the 20th century. In 1952, he won the 5,000 meters, the 10,000 meters, and the marathon at the Olympics in Helsinki. He was known as "The Locomotive."

Bob Beamon makes his record-breaking long jump that won him a gold medal on October 18, 1968, during the Olympics in Mexico City.

On the women's side, Jackie Joyner-Kersee has the all-time longest Olympic long jump at 24.3 feet (7.3 m). Joyner-Kersee is also considered one of the greatest all-around athletes ever. Along with her three Olympic medals in the long jump, she won another three in the **heptathlon**. The heptathlon is a track-and-field competition that combines seven different events. It includes the 100-meter hurdles, high jump, **shot put**, 200 meters, long jump, javelin, and 800 meters.

GREATEST OLYMPIC JUMPERS

EVENT	MEN	WOMEN
Long Jump	Bob Beamon (U.S.A., 1968): 29.2 feet (8.9 m)	Jackie Joyner-Kersey (U.S.A., 1988): 24.3 feet (7.3 m)
High Jump	Charles Austin (U.S.A., 1996): 7.84 feet (2.39 m)	Yelena Slesarenko (Russia, 2004): 6.76 feet (2.06 m)
Triple Jump	Kenny Harrison (U.S.A., 1996): 59.4 feet (18.09 m)	Francoise Mbango Etone (Cameroon, 2008): 50.4 feet (15.39 m)

MOST SUMMER OLYMPIC MEDALS

1. **Michael Phelps (U.S.A.): swimmer who won 22 medals**
2. **Larisa Latynina (Russia): gymnast who won 18 medals**
3. **Nikolai Andrianov (Russia): gymnast who won 15 medals**

Jackie Joyner-Kersee flies past Sierra Leone's Eunice Barber during the heptathlon 100-meter hurdles at the summer Olympics in 1996.

FASTEST PEOPLE IN THE WORLD

In 1988, Florence Griffith Joyner set the women's 100-meter dash record. Joyner was known as "Flo-Jo." She crossed the finish line in only 10.49 seconds. Her best time of 21.34 seconds in the 200-meter dash is also a world record.

During the 2008 Olympics, Jamaica's Usain Bolt ran faster than anyone ever had. He ran the 100-meter dash in 9.69 seconds. Bolt broke his own world record by .03 seconds. And he didn't even run the whole time. Toward the end of the race, Bolt looked around and realized no one was close behind him. He lifted up his arms and slowed his stride to celebrate. In 2012, he set the world record in the 200-meter dash as well.

STILL THE FASTEST MAN IN THE WORLD

At the 2012 summer games in London, Usain Bolt continued to outrun the competition. He won the gold in both the 100-meter dash and the 200-meter race. Bolt became the first man to win both races in two **consecutive** Olympics. His new 100-meter time was 9.63 seconds. It was a new Olympic record.

Sprinter Usain Bolt celebrates his new world record for the men's 100-meter dash at the 2008 Olympic games.

GREAT ATHLETES IN THE COLD

When the modern Olympics began in 1896, they only occurred in the summer. But in 1924 the Olympics became a winter event as well. Since then, the United States has won more winter Olympic medals than any other country. In 2010, short-track speed skater Apolo Ohno won his eighth Olympic medal. The athlete with the most winter Olympic medals is Norwegian cross-country skier Bjorn Daehlie. In three Olympics, he won a total of 12 medals.

MEDALISTS AT BOTH SUMMER AND WINTER OLYMPICS

ATHLETE	SUMMER	WINTER
Edward Eagan (U.S.A.)	Boxing: one gold	Bobsledding: one gold
Christa Luding-Rothenburger (Germany)	Track cycling: one silver	Speed skating: two golds, one silver, and one bronze
Jacob Thams (Norway)	Sailing: one silver	Ski jump: one gold
Clara Hughes (Canada)	Road cycling: two bronze	Speed skating: one gold, one silver, and two bronze

WORLD'S STRONGEST OLYMPIANS

One of the greatest tests of strength has one of the strangest names: the clean and jerk. In the clean and jerk, athletes lift a weighted bar from their knees to their shoulders. Then they push the bar above their heads. Hossein Rezazadeh of Iran has the Olympic and world record in the clean and jerk. In 2004, he lifted 580.9 pounds (263.5 kg).

MOST WINTER OLYMPIC MEDALS

1. Bjorn Daehlie (Norway): cross-country skier who won 12 medals
2. Ole Einar Bjoerndalen (Norway): biathlete who won 11 medals
3. Raisa Smetanina (Russia): cross-country skier who won ten medals

Bjorn Daehlie crosses the finish line to win the Olympic men's 10-kilometer classic style cross-country ski race on February 17, 1994.

THREE

MOST INSPIRING OLYMPIANS

Entering the 1988 winter Olympics, speed skater Dan Jansen was a favorite to win a gold medal. Hours before his race, though, he found out that his sister had died. Jansen's concentration was shattered. He fell on the ice during the race and did not win a medal. At the 1994 Olympics, Jansen slipped on the ice again. Over his career he set several world speed skating records, but it looked as though he might never earn an Olympic medal. His final Olympic race was the 1,000 meters in 1994. This time, Jansen did not fall or even slip. Not only did he earn his first medal, he took home the gold.

LONG-TRACK SPEED SKATING RECORDS

RACE	MEN	WOMEN
500 meters	Casey FitzRandolph (U.S.A., 2002): 34.42 seconds	Catriona Lemay Doan (Canada, 2002): 37.30 second
1,000 meters	Gerard van Velde (Netherlands, 2002): 1:07.18	Chris Witty (U.S.A., 2002): 1:13.83
1,500 meters	Derek Parra (U.S.A., 2002): 1:43.95	Anni Friesinger-Postma (Germany, 2002): 1:54.02

THE OLDER, THE BETTER!

In most sports an athlete has to be pretty young to succeed, but there are some sports where this is less the case. One of these sports is curling. In 1924, 54-year-old Robin Welsh of Edinburgh, Scotland, became the oldest male to win a gold medal in that sport.

Dan Jansen sets a new world record in the men's 1,000 meter race on February 18, 1994, at the Olympics.

A MARATHON RUN

According to Greek mythology, the first marathon was run by a Greek messenger. The messenger was racing to deliver urgent news about a nearby battle. He ran for 25 miles (40 km) from the town of Marathon to Athens. He finally arrived and delivered the message. The messenger's efforts were so amazing that the marathon race was named after the town from which he ran.

RECORD-BREAKING RUNS

At the 2012 summer Olympics in London, South African Oscar Pistorius ran in two events: the 400 meters and the 4x400 meter relay. He did not win either event, but his performances in both were still memorable. Pistorius is a double-**amputee**. He is missing both his legs from the knee down. Pistorius ran on **prosthetic** legs made of carbon. He became the first double-amputee to race in the Olympics.

MOST APPEARANCES IN OLYMPICS

ATHLETE	EVENT	TIMES IN THE OLYMPICS	YEARS
Ian Millar	equestrian	ten	1972–1976, 1984–2012
Hubert Raudaschl	sailing	nine	1964–1996
Afanaijs Kuzmins	shooting	nine	1976–1980, 1988–2012

BEST OLYMPIC MARATHONS

- **Men's record: Sammy Wanjiru (Kenya, 2008) with a time of 2:06:32**
- **Women's record: Tiki Gelana (Ethiopia, 2012) with a time of 2:23:07**

Oscar Pistorius competes in the men's 4x400-meter relay final at the 2012 London Olympics on August 10, 2012.

OLDEST SWIMMER

Viewers who watched Dara Torres at home during the 2008 summer Olympics may not have noticed anything different about her. Behind her goggles and cap, she looked a lot like the swimmers she raced against. If anything, she may have looked more muscular.

But Torres was different. For one thing, she was older than her competitors—by a long shot. She was also better than most of them. At the 2008 Olympics, at the age of 41, she won three silver medals. This made her the oldest swimmer to win a medal at the games.

AGELESS WONDER
At the 2006 winter games, 41-year-old Hilde Pedersen of Norway won a bronze medal in the 10-kilometer cross-country skiing race. The third-place finish made her the oldest woman to win an individual medal at the winter Olympics.

OLDEST OLYMPIC SWIMMING MEDALISTS

- **Women: Dara Torres (41)**
- **Men: William Robinson (38)**

Dara Torres prepares to start a women's 50-meter freestyle race during the Olympics on August 16, 2008.

FOUR

OTHER AMAZING OLYMPIC RECORDS

Oscar Swahn won his first Olympic medal when he was 60 years old. He won his last when he was 72. This was back in 1920, and some of the events were a little strange by today's standards. Swahn was a sharpshooter and won the silver medal in the running deer single-shot event.

In the 2012 Olympics, Hiroshi Hoketsu of Japan became the second oldest Olympian of all time at 71. Hoketsu competed in equestrian events.

FEMALE WITH MOST TOTAL MEDALS

The Soviet Union dominated gymnastics for decades. And the female gymnast who received most career medals was Larisa Latynina. Her career total was nine gold, five silver, and four bronze medals in three Olympic games.

Hiroshi Hoketsu rides his chestnut mare Whisper during an Olympic competition on August 2, 2012.

YOUNGEST OLYMPIANS

The youngest Olympian of all time competed at the very first modern Olympics in 1896. His name was Dimitrios Loundras, and he was only ten years old. The Greek gymnast was better than many adult athletes. He won a bronze medal that year in the team parallel bars.

There was another Olympian who may have been even younger. In 1900, a French boy helped a Dutch team win the gold medal in rowing, but nobody took the time to write down his name or his age. Historians believe he was somewhere between seven and 12 years old.

MORE SIZE RECORDS
- **Heaviest Olympian:**
  Ricardo Blas Jr. (judo) at 480 pounds (218 kg)
- **Smallest Medalist:**
  Lu Li (gymnastics) at 4 feet 5 inches (1.3 m)
- **Tallest Olympian:**
  Tom Burleson (basketball) at 7 feet 2 3/4
  inches (2.2 m)

Georgia's Lasha Gujejiani fights Guam's Ricardo Blas Jr. (white) in the judo men's heavyweight division at the 2008 Olympics on August 15, 2008.

THE STANDING HORSE JUMP

Of all the strange events at the Olympics over the years, one of the strangest was the long jump for horses in 1900. Many equestrian events continue to be a part of the Olympics, but there are good reasons for why this event is no longer part of the Olympic program. For one, the participants were not human. And the horses did not jump that far. In fact, they cannot jump from a standing position as far as humans can with a running start. The winning horse jumped more than 9 feet (2.7 m) less than the current human long jump record.

MOST EQUESTRIAN MEDALS

1. **Anky van Grunsven (Netherlands): nine medals**
2. **Reiner Klimke (Germany), Isabell Werth (Germany): eight medals each**
3. **Hans Gunter Winkler (Germany): seven medals**
4. **John Michael Plumb (U.S.A.), Josef Neckermann (Germany), Raimondo D'Inzeo (Italy), Piero D'Inzeo (Italy): six medals each**

Reiner Klimke won Olympic medals in dressage, an equestrian event, for Germany.

AN UNDERWATER OBSTACLE COURSE

Swimming events have been around as long as the Olympics. But not all of the swimming events have survived the last 100 years. One of the most interesting events in Olympic history only occurred once: the swimming obstacle course. In this event, athletes had to climb over a pole and a row of boats. Then they had to swim under a row of boats. In 1900, Australian Frederick Lane won the gold medal.

MOST CONSECUTIVE OLYMPIC GOLD MEDALS IN SAME INDIVIDUAL EVENT
- Carl Lewis (U.S.A.): four golds in long jump (1984, 1988, 1992, 1996)
- Alfred Oerter (U.S.A.): four golds in discus throw (1956, 1960, 1964, 1968)

Alfred Oerter competes
in the 1956 Olympics.

GLOSSARY

amputee (AM-pyuh-tee): An amputee is a person who has had an arm, finger, leg, or other part of the body removed because it is damaged or diseased. Oscar Pistorius is a double-amputee.

consecutive (kuhn-SEK-yuh-tiv): Something that is consecutive happens one after the other. Usain Bolt became the first man to win the 100-meter and 200-meter races in two consecutive Olympics.

discus (diss-KUHSS): A discus is a heavy disk that is thrown in a track-and-field event. Alfred Oerter won four golds in discus throw.

equestrian (i-KWESS-tree-uhn): An equestrian event is one that involves horseback riding. Hiroshi Hoketsu competed in equestrian events.

halteres (hul-TEERZ): Halteres are hand-held weights that were used to help athletes leap in ancient Greece. Athletes in ancient Greece threw halteres before they jumped in the long jump.

heptathlon (hep-TATH-lon): A heptathlon is a track-and-field competition made of seven different events. Jackie Joyner-Kersee won three medals in the heptathlon.

javelin (JAV-uh-luhn): A javelin is a light, metal spear that is thrown for distance in track-and-field events. The heptathlon includes a javelin throw.

prosthetic (pross-THET-ik): A prosthetic device is one that replaces a missing part of the body. Oscar Pistorius ran on prosthetic legs made of carbon in the 2012 Olympics.

shot put (SHOT PUT): Shot put is a track-and-field event in which a heavy ball is thrown as far as possible. The shot put is included in the heptathlon event.

LEARN MORE

Books

Butterfield, Moira. *The Olympics: Records.* Mankato, MN: Sea-to-Sea Publications, 2012.

Christopher, Matt. *Great Moments in the Summer Olympics.* New York: Little, Brown, 2012.

Kehm, Greg. *Olympic Swimming and Diving.* New York: Rosen Central, 2007.

Web Sites

Visit our Web site for links about Olympic records:
childsworld.com/links

Note to Parents, Teachers, and Librarians:
We routinely verify our Web links to make sure they are safe and active sites. So encourage your readers to check them out!

INDEX